MW01130198

The United States

Arizona

Paul Joseph

ABDO & Daughters

visit us at
www.abdopub.com

Published by Abdo & Daughters, 4940 Viking Drive, Suite 622, Edina, Minnesota 55435.
Copyright © 1998 by Abdo Consulting Group, Inc., Pentagon Tower, P.O. Box 36036,
Minneapolis, Minnesota 55435 USA. International copyrights reserved in all countries.
No part of this book may be reproduced in any form without written permission from the
publisher.

Printed in the United States.

Cover and Interior Photo credits: Peter Arnold, Inc., Super Stock

Edited by Lori Kinstad Pupeza
Contributing editor Brooke Henderson
Special thanks to our Checkerboard Kids—Stephanie McKenna, Matthew Nichols,
Francesca Tuminelly

All statistics taken from the 1990 census; The Rand McNally Discovery Atlas of The
United States. Other sources: Compton's Encyclopedia, 1997; *Arizona*, Heinrichs,
Children's Press, Chicago, 1989.

Library of Congress Cataloging-in-Publication Data

Joseph, Paul, 1970-
        Arizona / Paul Joseph.
        p. cm. -- (The United States)
        Includes index.
        Summary: Surveys the people, geography, and history of the Grand Canyon
        State.
        ISBN 1-56239-859-8
        1. Arizona--Juvenile literature. [1. Arizona.] I. Title. II. Series: United States
        (Series)
        F811.3.J67 1998
        979.1--dc21   97-910496
                                                             CIP
                                                             AC

Contents

Welcome to Arizona

Arizona is known as the Grand Canyon State because this beautiful scenic wonder lies in the northern part of the state. The spectacular Grand Canyon is a result of **erosion** by water and wind.

The state's name may have come from the Papago **Native American** word Arizonac, which means "little spring." The beauty of Arizona not only comes from the Grand Canyon, but also many other things. The state has tall, rugged mountains and clean, clear lakes.

Located in the Southwest, Arizona is bordered by Utah to the north, New Mexico to the east, and Mexico to the south. The Colorado River flows for almost the entire length of the western part of the state. The river separates Arizona from California and Nevada.

Arizona is almost square. From north to south its longest length is 395 miles (636 km). From east to west, its longest width is 343 miles (552 km). The Grand Canyon State is the sixth largest state in size.

This large state has splendid cities and wonderful natural treasures. It also has many **reservations** where **Native Americans** live.

Arizona's Grand Canyon.

Fast Facts

ARIZONA

Capital and largest city
Phoenix (983,403 people)

Area
113,510 square miles
(293,990 sq km)

Population
3,677,985 people
Rank: 24th

Statehood
Feb. 14, 1912
(48th state admitted)

Principal rivers
Colorado River
Gila River

Highest point
Humphreys Peak;
12,633 feet (3,851 m)

Motto
Ditat Deus
(God enriches)

Song
"Arizona"

Famous People
Cochise, Geronimo, Barry
Goldwater, Helen Jacobs, Sandra
Day O'Connor

*S*tate Flag

*F*lower of
Saguaro Cactus

*C*actusWren

*P*alo Verde

About Arizona

The Grand Canyon State

Detail area

AZ

Arizona's abbreviation

Borders: west (California, Nevada), north (Utah), east (New Mexico), south (Mexico)

Nature's Treasures

Arizona is known for its beauty. The Grand Canyon is in the northern part of the state. Mountains, plains, **deserts**, and gullies also make this state unique.

Almost half of the land in Arizona is owned by the United States. This means much of the land goes untouched. National and state parks make up a lot of this land.

Many years ago, gold and silver were the leading **minerals** in the state. Rich copper under the ground makes Arizona the biggest copper-**producing** state in the country and one of the biggest in the world. Arizona continues to rank high in gold, silver, and lead.

Northern Arizona has the biggest ponderosa pine forest in the United States. The state's most common trees are yellow pine, fir, and spruce.

Although Arizona is thought of as a **desert**, it also has rich farmland. There are many citrus farms, cotton farms, and truck farms.

The Grand Canyon State has wonderful rivers, beautiful lakes, and best of all, a fine climate. The dry, warm air goes very well with the beautiful scenery Arizona has to offer.

An Arizona copper mine.

Beginnings

The first **Europeans** to reach what is now Arizona were Spanish **explorers** and **missionaries** in the early 1500s. **Native Americans** were already living in Arizona. Among them were the Hopi, Papago, and Pima.

Marcos de Niza claimed the region for his native Spain in 1539. For almost 300 years the Spaniards continued to explore and make Arizona home. They brought **cattle**, horses, sheep, and new farming methods to the Native Americans.

The Treaty of Guadalupe-Hidalgo at the end of the Mexican War in 1848 gave the area to the United States. More wars broke out over the land. The Apache Wars lasted from 1865 until 1872. Many people were killed, including defenseless Native American women and children.

People from all over the country began coming to Arizona in the 1850s to strike it rich in gold. Gold was found along the Gila River. Copper became the most common **mineral** in Arizona.

While the mining and **cattle industries** were making money, the people living there wanted to make Arizona a state. On February 14, 1912, Arizona finally became a state. It was the 48th state out of 50 to join the Union.

An illustration of Native Americans during the time of Spanish exploration

Before 1500

The First People of Arizona

 Some of the first known people to live in the area now called Arizona were **Native Americans**. Among the Native Americans were the Hopi, Papago, and Pima.

 1125: Oraibi, the oldest Native American community, is founded in Arizona.

Arizona
Before 1500

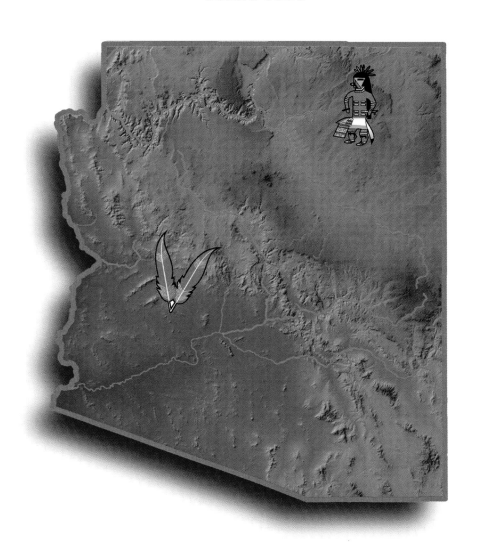

1500s to 1800s

New Arrivals

1539: Esteban guides Marcos de Niza through Arizona. Marcos claims region for Spain.

1540: Coronado and Marcos discover the Grand Canyon.

1580s: Antonio de Espejo finds silver near Prescott.

1821: Mexico creates New Mexico Territory and owns Arizona.

1863: United States creates the Arizona Territory. Fort Whipple is the capital.

14

Arizona

1500s to 1800s

1800s to Now

Statehood to Today

 1912: Arizona becomes the 48th state on February 14. Phoenix is the capital.

 1919: Grand Canyon National Park is opened.

 1936: The Hoover Dam is completed.

 1966: In the Miranda vs. Arizona case, the Supreme Court says that suspects must be told their rights. Today, it is called the Miranda Rights.

 1975: Raul Castro, the state's first Mexican-American governor is elected.

 1988: Arizona gets a professional football team: the NFL's Cardinals.

Arizona
1800s to Now

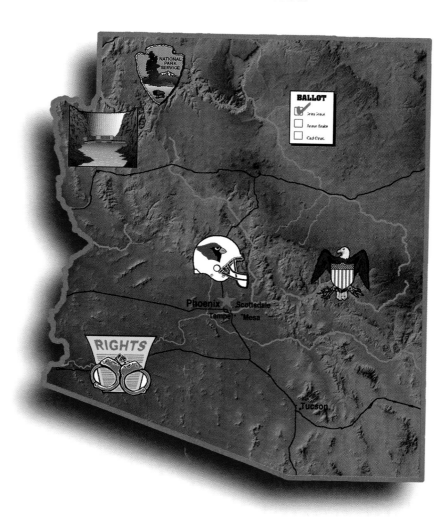

Arizona's People

Native Americans were the first people to live in Arizona. Spanish **explorers** and **missionaries** were the first **Europeans** to reach Arizona.

Today, there are about 3.7 million people in Arizona. Although most are white, African Americans and Native Americans make up about 10 percent of the people of Arizona. Some Native Americans live on the 20 **reservations** in Arizona.

Many well-known people have made the Grand Canyon State home. Raul Castro, born in Mexico, was the U. S. **ambassador** to El Salvador, Argentina, and Bolivia. In 1975, he was the first Mexican-American governor of Arizona.

Barry Goldwater was born in Phoenix. He was elected **senator** of Arizona in 1952. In 1964, he won the

Republican nomination for president of the United States. He lost the election, but was reelected to his senate seat in 1968.

Carl Hayden was one of the first representatives of Arizona when he was elected in 1912. In 1926, he was elected **senator** of Arizona. He served until 1969, setting a record for the most time served in the Senate.

Other notables include tennis great, Helen Hull Jacobs; composer Ulysses Kay; **explorer** and author Charles Poston; and singer Linda Ronstadt.

Navajo tribal fair, Arizona.

Splendid Cities

In general Arizona doesn't have a lot of cities. Each city, however, has much to offer. The biggest and best known city in Arizona is Phoenix, which is also the state capital.

Phoenix is a very important **industrial** city. It is a place for shipping crops, cotton, fruits, and beef. It is also a wonderful **resort** city. Phoenix has a lot of people that live there just in the winter to get away from the cold.

Tucson is home to about 400,000 people and is the second largest city in the state. It has a beautiful **desert** mixed with mountains. Many of the people who live in Tucson are students. One of the largest colleges, the University of Arizona, is in Tucson.

Just outside of Phoenix are cities like Mesa, Glendale, Tempe, Scottsdale, and Chandler. Each city is special in its own way. Each one gets many visitors in the winter because of the warm weather.

Downtown Phoenix, Arizona

Arizona's Land

Arizona's area is 113,510 square miles (293,990 sq km) including 364 square miles (943 sq km) of water surface. The Grand Canyon State is divided into two very different areas.

The Colorado Plateau is in the northern part of Arizona. It extends into Utah, Colorado, and New Mexico. This region is scarred by deep canyons and gullies. Snow-fed streams have been carving these for millions of years.

Mountain ranges, lofty peaks, and great flat-topped sandstone mesas stand tall in the Colorado Plateau. The Grand Canyon, Oak Creek Canyon, Painted **Desert**, and Petrified Forest are all in this region. Here too, is Humphreys Peak—the highest point in the state at 12,633 feet (3,851 m).

The Basin and Range Region is located in the southern and entire western part of Arizona. This area is made up of mountains and plains. The mountain section contains many **extinct** volcanoes. The mountaintops rise 4,000 to 6,000 feet (1,219 m to 1,829 m) above the valley floors. Below the mountains are plains, **deserts**, and valleys.

Grand Canyon National Park.

Arizona at Play

The people of Arizona enjoy the wonderful beauty of the state. The Grand Canyon State draws millions of visitors each year.

Arizona has more national parks and monuments than any other state. **Tourists** also visit the state's golf and tennis **resorts**.

People can visit **Native American** villages, dude ranches, and **desert** and mountain playgrounds. A person can walk, hike, or even ride horses through the Grand Canyon. Many just sit and stare at the natural beauty.

Arizona even offers excellent water sports. Whether it is swimming, boating, fishing, or skiing, Arizona has it. Lake Powell has remarkable rock formations in the middle of the lake.

If a person likes to just watch the action, Arizona offers that too. In professional sports there is the Phoenix Suns basketball team and Phoenix Cardinals football team. The state is also the place for many professional baseball spring training camps.

People in Arizona enjoy the outdoors.

Arizona at Work

The people of Arizona must work to make money. At one time Arizona's work was based on the "Four Cs"—copper, cotton, **cattle**, and citrus. Coal has recently been added.

Today **manufacturing** has become very important. Arizona's factories produce copper, processed foods, aircraft and aircraft parts, electrical equipment, and electronic equipment. Many thousands of people work in these factories.

Farmers work on the more than one million acres of land devoted to farming. The average farm size—4,700 acres—is the largest in the nation. Arizona ranks high in grapefruit and orange **production**.

A fine climate, beautiful scenery, and great outdoor sports make tourism a huge business in Arizona.

Because of all the visitors, many people work in service jobs. Service is working in stores, hotels, and restaurants for the people who visit Arizona.

One of Arizona's biggest money-makers is dude ranches. A dude ranch is a vacation **resort** that offers horseback riding and other fun things that western ranches would have.

Because of its beauty, people, and land, the Grand Canyon State is a great place to visit, live, work, and play.

Many people in Arizona work in the cattle business.

Fun Facts

•Arizona's first state capital was at Fort Whipple. One year later it was moved to Prescott. Finally, it was moved to Phoenix in 1889, where it still is today.

•The highest point in Arizona is Humphreys Peak. It is 12,633 feet (3,851 meters) tall.

•The lowest part of the state is the Colorado River at 70 feet (21 meters).

•Arizona is the sixth biggest state. It is 113,510 square miles (293,990 sq km).

Opposite page: The Colorado River in Arizona.

Glossary

Ambassador: a representative of one country who visits and lives in another country.

Cattle: farm animals such as cows, bulls, and oxen.

Desert: an area of land where there is little rain.

Erosion: being worn away slowly over time by water or wind.

European: people who originally come from countries in Europe such as England, Germany, Italy, etc.

Explorers: people that are one of the first to discover and look over land.

Extinct: no longer in use, alive, or working.

Farming: the business of working on a farm.

Industrial: big businesses such as factories or manufacturing.

Manufacture: to make things by machine in a factory.

Minerals: things found in the earth, such as rock, diamonds, coal.

Missionaries: people who carry on the work of a religious mission, often in a foreign country.

Native Americans: the first people who were born in and occupied North America.

Population: the number of people living in a place.

Production: what is grown or made for people to buy.

Reservations: an area of land where Native Americans live, work, and have their own laws.

Resort: a place to vacation that has fun things to do.

Senator: one of two elected officials from a state that represents the state in Washington D.C. There they make laws and are part of Congress.

Tourists: people who travel for fun.

Internet Sites

Arizonaweb
http://arizonaweb.org
A virtual Arizona Old-West town with a Saloon, Poker Palace, Bank, Town Hall, and a School.

Arizona's Web Hub
http://www.azwebhub.com
The WEBHUB is the biggest World Wide Web links covering information about Arizona as well as general-interest resources published by Arizona residents.

Kiosk Arizona
http://www.vii.com/~icis/kioskaz/home.htm
Catagorized links to Arizona Web resources: sports, arts, schools, weather, travel, cities, recreation, etc.

These sites are subject to change. Go to your favorite search engine and type in Arizona for more sites.

PASS IT ON

Tell Others Something Special About Your State

To educate readers around the country, pass on interesting tips, places to see, history, and little unknown facts about the state you live in. We want to hear from you!

To get posted on ABDO & Daughters website E-mail us at "mystate@abdopub.com"

Index